MILE MARKER 17

VERONICA CLAY

Featuring Poetic Pieces by

Isaac Clay, Shonyea Lind & Michaelah Weaver

Mile Marker 17

ISBN-13: 978-1-63110-267-7

Cover design by Kristina Clay

Author's photo by Sarah K Photography

Printed in the United States by
Mira Digital Publishing
Chesterfield, Missouri 63005

ACKNOWLEDGEMENTS

If you are reading this, you are my hero. Writing "Mile Marker 17" was just like that time I ran through church in the dark, smacked right into a metal pole, and cut my lip open on my braces (Yep. True story.) There have been many obstacles and, at times, I didn't think I would recover, but I made it!!! However, I would not be here today if it were not for everyone's love, support, and reprimands when I procrastinated. I thank God for blessing me with creativity and always loving me. My daddy and momma, Raymond and Kristina Clay, are pretty mind-blowing too. They have shaped me into the fierce, goofy, and wild child I am. They taught me that God didn't create me to fit in, but to be "unique, special, one of a kind." (It's an inside joke.) Isaac, my brother, has also been a huge help. He has pushed me to be better, told me not to take myself too seriously, and listened to my spoken words until he wanted to cut his ears off. Thanks, Scooter. My grandparents, Raymond, Cora, Jesse, and Mary Jo, are also pretty awesome. They are the O.G. Christians and have always prayed for me and supported me. "Ms. Hannah" is the bomb. She has mentored me in my writing and spiritual growth. Thanks for sticking with me through the most hormonal parts of my life, to-date. I am also grateful for Anthony Butler, author of "Fighting Words." He has guided me, checked on me, and reminded me to write, particularly when writing was the absolute last thing on my mind. I most certainly could not do it without Alane Watts, my super spy/millionaire. She teaches me to keep fighting, even when I don't know how the fight will end. Mackie (Michaelah Weaver) is also fantastic. She is talented, humble, and one of the goofiest people I have ever met. I will never forget the day I was no longer just her groupie, but her friend. Shonyea Lind, thanks for letting me coach you in writing. It was one of the most rewarding experiences. Your hard work paid off and now you're in a book! Love God and never give up on your dreams, Little One. Thank you every friend and family member who has supported me and prayed for me. You all are the best!

DEDICATION

Raymond, Kristina, and Isaac:

You encouraged me to write, even when I felt inadequate. You taught me to embrace my style of Spoken Word and to be true to myself. You believed in me, encouraged me, and put me first. I love you all and I could not have done any of this without you.

Contents

180

I wrote this spoken word when I was 13 years old. It is the first spoken word I ever created. I performed it at Sheffield Family Life Center in March of 2012. This spoken word was the breakthrough, so to speak. I realized, in creating and performing this piece, God gave me the gift of writing and speaking.

I lost myself

In this ever-wandering

Maze

I'm constantly amazed

That despite all this mess

You still call me Beautiful…

Was I fake God?

Was I just too unreal?

No

I made the choice

Not to feel

Or more like the choice

Of hiding so deep within myself

So heavily guarded

In a quiet place

I built the walls

High up around me

Forgetting about the life

1

That surrounds me

The seed—

It was planted two years ago

I was mocked

I was criticized

But instead of turning the other cheek

Like Jesus did

I uttered spiteful words

That to this day

I regret

And of course

I apologized

But the devil wouldn't let me forget

he whispered,

"This is what happens when you are yourself

You hurt people

You hurt God"

I didn't realize it was him

But I withdrew from the world

Hiding

From what I felt

Was an unforgivable sin

It happened slowly

Over the years

But I kept my thoughts

My opinions

And who I was

To myself

When my best friend and I grew apart

It broke my heart

She was the one person

I felt free with

Like I could be me with

When she left

Everything started to cave in

Collapsing

But I kept it quiet

When tears wanted to fall

I blocked them

When a strong feeling came

I stopped it

To you

I would look strong

These are the shoulders you'd rely on

You would call me courageous

But if you looked inside

You'd find

It outrageous

Because under all of this bravery

Is fear

But don't worry

It's not contagious

And don't think I wasn't living by the Holy Pages

I was still saved

But I didn't feel free

I felt bound by the chains of captivity

And I felt the weight

As I dragged those chains

Covered in all of their

Tormenting pains

I thought,

"This must be the pain of life"

But no

That can't be right

Jesus said "Be free"

So why do I feel like there's a cage around me?

He said,

"I forgive thee"

But to truly understand the beauty

4

You have to hear me

I cried

"God!

These chains

These fears

Why are they here?"

I had this phobia

Of being me

Because I was afraid

I would hurt everyone

I touch and see

But what He said

Was just enough

He said

"Never will I leave you

Never will I forsake you

I made you

How could I ever hate you?"

He took my life

And with a spin

He turned it around

And it wasn't that I was in

The wrong place

Full of sin

He made my life better

From within

I refuse to hide

I hate those lies

So shut up Satan!

Go back to Hades

God loves me

God made me

He turned my life around 180

He's my God

My Savior…

I give all my thanks to Thee

My Jehovah Nissi

Your banner flies over me

You're my pops

My best friend

Devotion

I wrote this spoken word when I was 13 years old in 2012. I created this piece while I was on the eFAM Writing Team of my youth group, eMPAKT.

Devotion:

The how to options

Are greater than an ocean

But it all comes down to one thing

You and God

Sometimes

We forget that He's there

We chase life

Without a worry or care

But then there's that fork in the road

You look back

And see you've reaped what you've sowed

You look again

You don't know which way to go

You don't have a clue

On who to ask

Or what to do

So you look in the mirror

Remembering the days

When things were clearer

When was that?

Back then life was sunny

And things were better

Now there's just clouds

And you keep on getting wetter

You feel like you've aged

Desperation creeps

And you're left alone caged

And then you remember

It was 2010

Sometime in December

You didn't spend time with God

You saw the price

But didn't understand the cost

It's taken you 'til now

To realize what you've lost

Your world's in jeopardy

It's worse than back in the Bible days

When people had leprosy

You're in the damp dark

Alone and cold

All the fun and living high

Starts getting old

You brush back the cobwebs of your memory

And see that it was worthless

You wish you could rewind

And tell yourself it wasn't worth this

You think back

And then you're positive

And with a nod

You whisper out loud,

"I wish I would have stuck with God"

You gaze back with a tear streaked stare

You left devotions long ago

On some dusty old chair

As if they didn't matter

But in truth

It was Death or Life

And now you wish you chose the latter

And you start getting madder

Wishing you chose to climb the ladder

All the way to heaven!

But instead you sat back

Too complacent to spend time with God

As though you were seven

This looks like a sad ending

Wish you wouldn't have spent so much time

Facebook-friending

So now you start sending

Out the S.O.S.

Now you wish you would have given

God your best

From small devo's

To true devotion

You look back

And as if watching in slow motion

You realize

They are number one

Greater than parties

Above all fun

They could even save you

From the suicidal thoughts you have in your room

When you're tempted to hold up that gun

And just end it…

Spending time with God

Is most important

If we don't have time

Let's make it

But let's not sit back

And fake it

Jesus gave us Life

And saved it!

Shouldn't we take some time

To thank Him?

If you devote to spending time with God

I know you won't hate it

You'll drink in True Life

And be full

Sated

Your life

Jesus took His time

And made it

Don't you think we should

Appreciate it?

Devotions

It's more than a book

It's more than a prayer

It's spending time

With the True God up there

It will turn your life around

I swear

Neighbors

This rap was written when I was 14 years old and my brother, Isaac, was 11 years old. We created it for the Fine Arts Festival in 2013 and were invited to Nationals. The verse for that year's festival was Acts 20:24, which we recited at the beginning of the song, after the Mr. Rogers Neighborhood *theme song played.*

Verse 1 (Veronica)

No more depression

I'm feeling freshened

No more shyness

I met His Highness

No more dark fear

It's been made clear

But hold up

Let me rewind this

I am a girl who was saved from death

Ice cold hands choked me

Tried to take my breath

I blacked out

Flash back to the past

All that foolish indulgence

Really thought it would last

Mistakes—no sin

All of it was blatant

World had me acting stupid like Satan

'Til every part of me

I really started hating

'Cause every part of me

Knew that I was faking

Thank God He reopened my eyes

Made me so clean

That I didn't recognize me

Now I'm unashamed

Can't nobody hide me

And my God's right here

Arms open saying, "Try Me"

Chorus

So if you want to be our neighbor

Step up it's time to meet Our Savior

Acts 20:24 yea were some of them racers

We ain't stopping 'til you met Our Creator

We'll take you to Our Leader

We'll take you to Our Maker

We ain't stopping 'til you met Our Creator

We'll take you to Our Leader

We'll take you to Our Maker

Let the world hear The Lord

They can't stop us

Verse 2 (Isaac)

Finishing this race

And nah I ain't gonna hesitate

The Lord He got my back

His grace and mercy gonna penetrate

I ain't trying to procrastinate

Been running since six

All the way to the present date

This race is crazy

I ain't gonna be lazy

Been running my whole life

And my vision ain't hazy

You know I'm running around

Screaming Jesus is King

He made me

And maybe He deserves some praise, see

In this race

You gotta keep a steady pace

It gets hard to keep

Control over your faith

In this thing

The goal is to chase

The One who has

The ultimate grace

Blazing while I'm racing

And I'm praising cause His grace

And His love I'm embracing

And there ain't no replacing

And the thought

Of His glory

Can't be erased

And His love over me is like a protective casing

(Chorus)

Verse 3 (Part One—Veronica)

'cause my God is real

And He's got us slaying dragons

It ain't no magic word

It's 'cause of God

We be swagging

To some of y'all here

It may appear as though we're bragging

But we're bragging on our God

That's why we're standing here rapping right?

Listen up to the word of the day

It ain't too late to apologize like One Republic say

God forgives the sinner

Who gets on his knees and prays

That's why I'm here today

Able to say what I say

Verse 3 (Part Two—Isaac)

I'm supposed to tell the world

Of His goodness and glory

His life represents

The most perfect story

Kind of like Judas

We treat God poorly

But we gotta repent and keep on soaring

You know what I gotta finish

What I shine

Can't be diminished

There's a fire in my heart

And it can't be extinguished

My life is easy – to be distinguished.

Heaven-Bound

I wrote this poem when I was 15 years old. I had to create a few lines of iambic pentameter for my high school English class, but I decided to make an entire poem. I dedicate this to great grandmother, Velma McCaffery, and my grandfather, Kenneth Faulkner, who went to be with the Lord.

Their hearts grew wings and wished the world good-bye.

No more attached by strings, they learned to fly.

They laugh and dance with clouds that pass them by

And rest among the stars of the night sky.

No longer weak, they sing with all their might

And wonder at the world. Oh! Such a sight!

Their hearts await the day of true delight,

When you grow wings and join them in their flight.

Limitless

I wrote this rap when I was 15 years old. I wrote it as the second verse in a Rap Group for the Fine Arts Festival in 2014. This group placed first at Districts and fourth at the National Fine Arts Festival.

I want to be fearless

Maybe you can feel this—

I'm filled with insecurity

I need to let God heal this

I want to shine Christ's light

In my own way

But I'm afraid that I'll fail—

Then what will people say?

I was afraid that if I failed

God couldn't love me

I'd be an outcast

Everybody'd judge me

But I find that this viewpoint is flawed

It doesn't matter what they say

'Cause my judge is God

And He will never stop loving me

God plus me equals forever—infinity

So I find my identity

In He who created me

Share what He's given me

With God they can't limit me

Anxiety and fear used to chain me

God broke them chains—

With Him they can't contain me

The ex-masters wonder "Where's the slave?"

"Bro it aint me!"

Thanks to my Limitless God I'm set free.

Different

I wrote this spoken word when I was 15 years old in January of 2014. I created it to fit the Fine Arts Festival theme of "Limitless." This was the first year I competed in the spoken word category at this competition. I won Merit Award (first place) at Districts and received an invitation to Nationals.

From a distance

I would look pretty normal

Walking on two feet

Having two hands

Each with five fingers

I'm an active

Church attendee

And a worship singer

But I dance

To the beat

Of a different drum

I'm the sound of

Melodies

And harmonies

That have never been sung

I tell people,

"I am different because of God"

But they don't like my

Explanation

So a lot of times

The word "different"

Earns a negative

Connotation

But I'm not the only one

Who is different

Example A:

In the left corner

Is Goliath

The Philistines'

Favorite giant!

Nine feet tall

The size of a king

And in the right corner is

David…

Why is he even in this ring?

Yet David

Wasn't the one decapitated

Rather

Through God

He won

Leaving all of Israel's enemies

Hating

Better yet

Look at Esther

The Queen of Persia

How could the circumstances

Get any better?

Yet her

People were going to face

Annihilation

So she willing

Threw down

All self-preservation

And admitted

She was a Jew

And that

She was different

Even though the king

Could take her life

In an instant

She was fighting

For her people to live

So like Christ

Her life she did give

Yes

Her very life

22

Was on the line!

But the favor of King Xerxes

And God

She did find

What about another hero?

Born A.D.

Zero

Jesus

He completed

The greatest rescue mission

Ever performed

He succeeded

Because He wasn't willing

To conform

But be different

He grew up

With favor in many eyes

But while reaching out to people

He was hated

And despised

He grasped those

Some could never think

Of touching

He loved those

23

Some could never dream

Of loving

He was compassionate

Funny

Kind

He most definitely didn't fit in

But His love

For God and us

Made Him

Okay

With being different

Think about how many times

He thought of quitting

How much His heart ached

Surly He wanted to give in!

But no

He continued His quest

To save the liars

And perjurers

The adulterers

And murderers

The likes

And all the rest

He gave His all

And nothing less

So that we

Could receive

His very best

Distinct, Individual

Off-beat, Peculiar

Opposed

All these words vary

Yet have the same meaning

Or goal

In the same way

All of us are unique

Yet we have the same purpose

In our soul

To creatively give glory

To God

Yet so many times

We get caught

Chasing someone else's story

So now the majority

Has become dull

And the heroes are those

Who are willing to be full

Of bravery

Honor

Love

And a willingness

To stand out

When everyone else is quiet

The strength to be loud

Now look at your index finger…

No I'm serious

Notice all the loops and lines

All the swoops and winds

Every single finger print

Is of individual design

Every single hand

Is like a sign

That implies

That the Great Creator

Took the time

To make you special

One of a kind

We are supposed

To be different

That is how we shine

Christ's light through the dark

So yea

Some people call me weird

Or different

But I prefer to say

I'm set apart

For the **LIMITLESS**.

The Battle Cry

I wrote this rap when I was 15 years old. I created it for the Fine Arts Festival in 2014. This was the first solo rap I wrote and performed.

I am compelled by Love to finish it

Filled with Jesus' Spirit can't no one diminish it

This changes everything; He changed my life

So lift your candles up like forty men on thin ice!

What? Uh, excuse me—a lesson in history

Roman Empire in the early fourth century

Ruler said, "I am god; worship me

Disown your Christ and you will all go free"

Well 40 soldiers—they disobeyed

"Disown Jesus the Christ? Uh, No Way"

Ruler says, "Well, it's winter. There's a frozen lake

Their will may be strong but how much can their bodies take?"

Each man, stripped naked, candle in hand

Sat on the ice—He was a follower Not a Fan

'Cause 40 men refused to bow down

In the morning 40 bodies on the ice were found

But this is not the end of their story

'Cause 40 men in heaven are sharing in glory

And through their death, they shared The Light

'Cause God made them strong to push through and fight.

If they shared Christ, so why can't we?

Let's break up chains, set captives free

If God fights for us with power that's endless

Our victory's eternal…limitless

Chorus

This is a battle

But don't ever lose hope

'Cause we know that we win

And it'll be worth it in the end

I know it's hard times

But we got to share His Light

So I'll trust Him with all of me

'Cause I know that He holds the victory

Verse 2

We don't fight flesh and blood

But demonic principalities

So when my fists ain't up

Know it's not man that I'm battling

But the darkness that controls them

Telling them that victory is hopeless

Well demons choke this; you already know this

Victory is given to all those who know Him

So in the end, we win 'cause He sent

His Son to become the ultimate sacrifice

War's already won; we no longer have to die

There's Life in His Son, so I'mma be on His side

Because of His Love, I stand up and fight

Advancing God's Kingdom, show the world His Light

And if you listening and you take interest

If you ain't a Christian—consider this enlistment

'cause the truth is we all sin we all fall

God still wants us, will you answer the call?

The Rescue

I wrote this sonnet when I was 15 years old. I created it for the Fine Arts Festival in 2014. The poem reveals one of my greatest fears and depicts God rescuing me from that fear.

I'm scared to death of you

Your jaws are gaping wide

From your claws I try to hide

How to flee from you, I wish I knew

Because of you I'm afraid to do

Those things that make me smile

Those things could be worthwhile

But I'm scared to death of you

For only God can save me from

This self-inflicted dreg I drink

He cures the ache from which I ail

And rescues me from death to come

So to the dirt my soul won't sink

For He removes my fear to fail.

Made to Love

I wrote this 8 bar rap when I was 15 years old. I created it for Empakt's purity series, "Made to Love." I performed it in the spring of 2014 to the song "Wake" by Hillsong Young and Free with the eMPAKT worship team.

You will never fade away

You're in my heart

And You're here to stay

You remain the same

You're an anchor to my soul

You're the God who saves

You're my loving hope

Because of You

We can get free

Show the world

How it should be

It's time to shine

Bright like the sun

Let's show KC

We were made to love

American Freedom

I wrote this spoken word when I was 15 years old. I performed this at the World War I Museum in Kansas City, on June 27, 2014 for the Missouri Veterans Commission Ceremony honoring World War II and Korean War Veterans.

American Freedom

What is the first thing

That comes to mind

When attempting to describe

This attribute

Is it red, white, and blue?

Is it camouflage

And badges?

Or maybe the lack

Of receiving lashes?

What feelings come to mind?

Happiness?

Patriotism?

Thankfulness?

But for some of us

I imagine

These feelings of appreciation

Aren't always long lasting

Why?

Maybe because we are like fish in water

Swimming in this free atmosphere

That hardly ever falters

It is hard to imagine slavery

When freedom's all we've known

Or bondage

When grace

Is all we've ever been shown

We can become so self-absorbed

Living in our own little world

That we forget

That we are blessed

Living in a land of providence

When there are others

With so much less

We have the divine rights of Life

Liberty

And the Pursuit of Happiness

Our lives aren't perfect

But compared to the third world

They're slightly fabulous

But the most important quality

Of American Freedom

Is the opportunity

To pursue true

Freedom

Now some of you may be thinking,

"If I am free,

Why would I need more freedom?

What else could I possibly be seeking?"

How many of you

Though free

Feel chained

Depression arising

At the rise of another day

Or anxiety screaming in your face

Have you ever felt incomplete?

You're not fully free

Though technically not enslaved

Living life wondering

"What's the point?"

Pondering

Life's true meaning

But not sure how to voice your questions

Being free

And yet enslaved

Because our American Freedom

Hasn't yet met completion

The original reason

For the establishment

Of the American Kingdom

Was for the receiving

Of religious freedom

The reason

We left Spain, France, and England

Was because we could not stay

We longed for a land

To worship God

In our own way…

Freedom

It comes in two parts

Freedom of the body

And freedom of the heart

Physical freedom

We have thoroughly achieved

Though spiritual freedom

Some of us have not received

How many of you long for a life

Where joy is regular

And peace is common?

Where laughter and comfort

Flow freely like a fountain

How many long for scars to be erased

Your biggest fears

To be faced

And defeated

Because victory

Is on your side

No matter where you go

And hope is in your heart

Even when you've reached the lowest of lows

A life where protection is offered

Without using Allstate

And guidance is given

Through the knots in your life's maze

A life that isn't yet perfect

But only improving

True perfection ensuing

Meaning

It's coming

A day when no tears

Will fall from our faces

And no sorrow

Will be in our hearts

A day where the grave

Is no longer tasted

And pain will no longer

Tear us apart

A day of true and entire victory

For some of you

I am pulling on your heart strings

And with words

Creating a symphony

As you picture a life painted beautifully

What if I told you

This reality

Is true for me

And that this masterpiece

Is how life is supposed to be

Jesus Christ

Gave His life

To set us free

He loved us so much

That He was willing to be crucified

But death lost the three day match

And watched Him rise

But Christ didn't just do this

For all humanity

He did it for you and me personally

So that each one of us

If we believe

Would be able to receive

Eternal life

American Freedom

It's what millions have died for

The opportunity to seek Him

And to live

In God's Heavenly Kingdom

But it's not just for then

It's for now

It's for kids

To be able to play in their backyards

Safe and sound

It's for children

To run on sidewalks

Chasing fireflies

Instead of being filled with fear

And having to hide

You stepped out of your homes

With uncertainty

Of returning to your husbands, children, and wives

To ensure the security

Of American rights

You risked your lives

To protect ours

And whether you were drafted

Or enlisted

And you readily consented

You protected American peace

And contentment

You risked your lives

Making a selfless sacrifice

And we are indebted

We honor this sacrifice

May we never forget it

From the Army,

Navy

And Marine Corps

To the Coast Guard

And Air Force

I personally thank you

For your service

And I pray that God will bless

You and America

The land

Of the free

And the home

Of the brave

After the Rain

This song was written by Michaelah Weaver in summer of 2014. She asked me to write a rap to her song and I was incredibly excited. I wrote two verses about my mother's childhood. I was 15 years old at the time.

Chorus

So lift your head up

Open up your eyes

Oh the light may sting,

But the truth hurts

When all you've heard is lies

Don't you worry

Don't be afraid

Flowers only grow after the rain

Flowers only grow after the rain

Verse 1

I met a girl with a broken past

She had a family but it didn't last

Alcohol and abuse

Was what she knew as a kid

She heard the banging and the yelling

From the room where she hid

She faced things

That little girls shouldn't have to face

And all the pain

Made her heart into a broken place

Her parents separated

A half-brother on his way in

And now a new man

To take her father's place

She might have thought,

"How can God have plans for me?

When I can't even have

A whole and happy family?"

But now she's twenty-three

And got two kids

And the babbies' daddy

He's her husband

She realized

That only with God

Could she really make it

And as a family

You need God's strength to take it

And now she knows

That she is never on her own

Even when the world caves in

She is not alone

So the storm may come

And rage all around

But flowers only grow

After the rain has touched the ground

So her life as a kid

Was a catastrophe,

But God touched her story

And turned it into a masterpiece

Verse 2

Now she would say,

"I'm still filled with insecurities

But never fear

For I know

That my God is healing me

And by His grace

I have a whole family

I don't have to fear for

He is taking care of me

'Bout eighteen years

Since the start of this family

And we will stick together

To the end of eternity

So to my momma,

Who used to sing me lullabies

One day He will wipe

Every tear from your eyes

You faced the storm and

You felt the tide but

Don't be afraid 'cause

God is always on your side

So highly favored

Child of The One King

It's time to sing before the throne

And let God set you free.

Native

I wrote this piece when I was 15 years old at the request of Pastors Austin Westlake and Burt Taylor Jr. of Sheffield Family Life Center. I performed it on, September 17, 2014, in honor of the launch of the new youth group, Native Youth Kansas City (NYKC). I specifically created it to explain the three goals of NYKC: RETURN, RECLAIM, and REMAIN.

My people,

Here we are existing

But not really living

Being

But not truly seeing

And believing

In our potential

We have been bound by captivity

For far too long

But our chains have been broken

Our captors have all gone

It is time to **RETURN**

To our Native Land

To the palm of God's hand

To The One who loves us so much

He willingly chose to die

To give us a rich and satisfying life

45

It is time to **RECLAIM**

The plan

That was given to each individual man

Intended from the beginning

But lost due to birth

In a world

Sick with sinning

It is time we take back

What is rightfully ours

Our hopes and dreams

Reaching beyond the stars

The plans created

By the Ultimate Designer

Who is our purpose

And destiny definer

The plan, like a map

Directs us where to go

He says,

"For I know the plans I have for you

And they are plans of hope"

And finally

We must **REMAIN**

We must finish this race

Pressing on to the ending

Never looking back

But only forwardly ascending

To our true and holy

Native Land

To heaven on earth

The ultimate finish to His plan

A finish that is infinitely perfect

And eternally lasting

But before we reach the final victory

We must continue battling

To **RETURN**

To our Native Land

To **RECLAIM**

His perfect plan

And to **REMAIN**

In our Father's hand

From now on

All of us are warriors

And it is time to take a stand

You are not just a messenger

But a defender

Of our Native Land

My people,

We have been bound by captivity

For far too long

It is time to end our futility

And begin our battle song.

Stamp F

I wrote this spoken word when I was 15 years old. I created it for Ashley Griffin to dance to in October of 2014. She danced to it and won second place in the Miss Black and Gold Pageant at the University of Missouri-Kansas City.

You've been there right?

In the moment

It felt so good

And seemed so acceptable

But now

In the middle of the night

As you lie

In your bed

You've never felt so detestable

You feel like it's over

And impossible

For you to change

Your biggest addiction

Is your biggest shame

And of course

You tried to break it

But it only broke you

You realize

Your lust and desire

49

Is bigger than your resolve to change

You will always be the same

Stamp F

For Failure

At least

These were my thoughts

When attempting cold turkey

Every time I failed

I felt so unworthy

And so weak

But what if I told you

That is exactly what we

Are

Incapable of accomplishing

Any spiritual feat

We are unable to dawn righteousness

By our own attempts

Stamp F

For Failure

"All have sinned

And fall short of the glory of God"

But I would try to be religious

And give it all I got

But I only fell further

And it was only in my deepest

Darkest

Moment

When my heart was so broken

That through the cracks

It was actually open

To let down my pride

And realize

I couldn't do it

I could not redeem my past

I could not fix my problems

I understood

"All have sinned

And fall short of the glory of God"

But **READ ON**

"And are justified freely

By His *grace*

Through the redemption

(Or payment)

That came in

By Christ Jesus"

Most people reject Christianity

And Christ

Because they don't feel good enough

They know they can't measure up

They feel imperfect

There's no way

Some Guy

Would die

For them

They just aren't

Worth it

But you see

Ephesians 2:8-9 says,

"For it is by **GRACE**

You have been saved

Through faith

And this not from yourselves

It is the gift of God"

A gift of grace

Grace is defined

As a manifestation of favor

Especially by a superior

You may say,

"If I can't earn it

How can I have favor

If I don't deserve it?"

Simple

Jesus loves you so much

That He willingly chose

To hang on the cross

Because to Him

You were worth it

You could not pay for yourself

So He took out a check

Signed His name in blood

And paid your debt

Because He deemed you

Worth it

"For I am convinced

That neither death

Nor life

Neither angels

Nor demons

Neither the present

Nor the future

Nor any powers

Neither height

Nor depth

Nor anything else in all creation

Will be able to separate us

From the love of God

That is in Christ Jesus

Our Lord"

I used to stamp F

For Failure

I thought I'd always be addicted

And never satisfied

But I heard by grace

There is life

In Christ Jesus

So I took a leap of faith

And believed Him

God broke my chains

And changed my life

Now

I stamp F

For Freedom.

The Fairy Tale

I wrote this spoken word when I was 16 years old in celebration of the marriage of Kenny and Hannah McDaniel. I performed it at their magical wedding on November 29, 2014.

"Every person's life

Is a fairy tale

Written by God's fingers"

-Hans Christian Anderson.

As a child

One grows up believing

In true love

And fairy tales

In heroic knights

And cunning princesses

Only to grow older

And be told

That this amazing life

Does not exist

That it

Is impossible

However

May these words

Never come from the mouth of a Christian

For it is through Christ

That the impossibly

Beautiful tale

Is woven

Such as this very instance

For here and now

In this very moment

A magic so deep

So strong

And more powerful

Than the ocean

Has swept

Through the room

Its current flowing

In our hearts

Because in this moment

Heaven kisses earth

In this moment

God's perfect plan

Is accomplished

Once upon a time

There was a pure daughter

And a pure son

Their eyes were opened

By God

That before them

Was the one

He prepared for them

Before time began

And realizing

In wonder

The beauty and strength

They found in each other

They fell in love

Not in a mere

Infatuation

But a true love

In a love

That every day

Would grow stronger

And this strength

Would help them go farther

Until together

They would reach

The end of time

And victoriously cross

The finish line

Right here

In this magical moment

Their journey has begun

A fairy tale

Yet to be sung

So rejoice friends!

Rejoice

Oh brothers of the groom!

For your friend

Who has found a wife

Has found

Good things

He has found a treasure

Far greater than diamonds

Pearls or gold

For it is a crown of joy

That she brings

Rejoice oh friends

You sisters of the bride!

For she has patiently waited

And God has blessed her

With a good life

He has blessed her

With a husband,

A leader,

A protector

They each could have gone

Their own way

But they trusted

That God knew better

Thus a virtuous and precious woman

A princess

Has been found by a prince

Noble and chivalrous

Rejoice!

For the blessing of God

Is upon them

Be proud and honored

Give glory to God

Parents of this son

And daughter!

You have raised

Them well

You have taught them

God's ways

You have blessed them

With the chance

To together

Seek His face

To live

A blessed life

And to dance

In His grace

So all of you shout

And sing!

Let every eye see

The fairy tale come true

In this bride

And groom

See how God

Has adorned them!

In this very moment

His smile is upon them

Let us sing!

Let us dance!

Let us celebrate!

For here and now

A new fairy tale begins

And while we do not

Know the end

We know the Author

So we know that they'll live

Happily ever after.

Shift

I wrote this spoken word when I was 16 years old. I created it at the request of Pastor Kevin Brown for the launch of "Shift," the young adult ministry of Sheffield Family Life Center. I performed it at Shift's launch service on January 18, 2015.

Imagine

A world

Always ravaged

By storms

A world that knows very little light

Even less refuge

And you

Have lived your whole life

Bearing the storms

Abuse

The rain beats

As lightning flashes

The wind screams

And thunder roars

But from a distance

Someone with a candle calls

Your name

And you make

Up your mind

To *shift*

And follow

He grabs your hand

Pulls you into a shelter

Rescuing you from the weather

You have never

Known a place

Where you could feel safe

Until now

Times passes

And you begin to realize

That you are like

A child

Who has returned

To his Father

This is a love

That could never falter

One day

Very soon

Lying on the table

Are tools

Which he

Teaches you how to use

Until you're strong enough

To handle them

And as though

There were a passing of the mantle

He hands you

A piece of His hearth

In the form of a candle

And you

Remember the storm

In which you were found

The sound

And memories flood in

And you

Now equipped

Shift

Take the tools

And begin

To build

Although the wind howls

And rain batters down

You have a purpose

And are driven

You won't stop

Until you're finished…

You place your candle

In this tower

You built a lighthouse

To shine through the rain showers

The light spreads

Hope is sent

On for leagues

As people begin to *shift* and see

The light that you shine

And when they find—it

They find a chance

For something more

Than survival and rain

So they stay

And when the broken enter in

They feel peace

And are free

They are

Home at last

But just like you realized

You had a purpose

So, when they arrive

They too

Unearth this

That they are indebted

And grateful servants

And they can't help

But do good works—so

They build lighthouses

And shining towers

To guide the lost to a city

Shielded from the storm's power

Thus the cycle continues:

They are equipped to build

They reach the lost

Thus arises

A city on a hill

—A community of people

Who serve and help

The battle-worn warriors

Who need a home

And these begin to hone

Their skills

And are equipped to build

They reach the lost

Then arises

Another city on a hill

—A community of people

Who serve and help

The battle-worn warriors

All this began

With the man

Who was the candle carrier

He painted this picture

Of redemption

Where those who enter

Find home

And learn to know

That they are not alone

And as they grow

That they are meant

To be so much more

Than battle-torn

Is what they discover

They learn to love Him

Who is the Light-Giver

And each other

The light shines in their eyes

And these conquerors

Grow in numbers

They've all tasted

The dark storm

But now

They know the light

And that hope can't be undone

They are an unstoppable family

Who are united

Willing and ready to fight

For a life

That is much better

Than what their world promises

They do not conform

But stand out

Because The Light

Showed them how

They are not willing

To remain stagnant

But are moving

In a constant

March forward

They are different

They shine far brighter than the norm

Because they were willing to *shift*

They will change the world.

Fearless Life

I wrote this rap when I was 16 years old for the Fine Arts Festival of 2015. I participated in the Rap Group category with Isaac Clay and Shonyea Lind. Isaac assisted with the sound and hook production. We placed fourth in the National Fine Arts Festival.

Verse 1 (Shonyea)

Since I was younger

My mom was like thunder

She blew up in my face

But I never knew what for

I thought it could be me

Or maybe my sister

The drugs had taken her

Just like a twister

I was left alone 'til 12 A.M.

Never did sleep

Felt the paranoia

And anxiety

Never thought I'd make it

Not through the pain

Never thought I would be living to this day

I was so tired

Just wanted it to end

Felt so alone—

Didn't really have friends

Wasn't a believer

Didn't know Christ

Not until my new parents stepped into my life

God was with me through the troubled

The good and the bad

Now I can say

He's really got my back

I'm unashamed

Unafraid

Don't want to hide

Wanna share the gospel—

Show that God's in my life

Hook (2x)

If you ain't scared

Let me see your hands up

If you finna go

Let me see your hands up

The time is now

Gotta spread "The Human Right"

Let 'em know

With God we got that fearless life

Verse 2 (Veronica)

Guts over fear

And now I see clear

It's not about me

I'm done lookin' in the mirror

No more obsession

'Bout what people will think

"What if they don't like me

Or the words that I speak?"

I'm done hiding behind

A fake humility

It's just anxiety

'cause I don't trust the God inside of me

But now I'll be

Strong and courageous

Step up to the mic

And rock any stages

Not because of who I am

But because of who He is

God's got your girl

So now I walk it out with confidence

It should be obvious

That I put my trust in Him

Who should I fear

When He's got the world in His hands?

I got gifts

And I need to utilize them

No time for hiding

Shine bright like a diamond

The sky's the limit

So I spread my wings

Leave the cage

I'm done with fear

Now it's time to flip the page

Hook (2X)

Bridge (2x)

With God inside

Who should I be scared of?

He got me like "ha!

Come at me bruh!"

Hook (2x)

The King's Child

I wrote this poem when I was 16 years old. I created it for the Fine Arts Festival of 2015 and received the rating of "Superior with Invitation to Nationals."

I am a rebel—a treacherous traitor.

I once was a child who sat at the King's table.

In war, I traded my freedom for treason.

I battled and ravaged my Father's great kingdom,

But I was a fool for my leader betrayed me.

He'd always intended to hurt and enslave me!

For months how I yearned to be free—to be rescued!

I dwelled on my old life and what it had come to

When all of a sudden, in thunder and glory

The King then appeared and He headed right toward me!

He cut down the soldiers and all opposition.

He broke off my chains and took in my condition.

But I, so ashamed, looked away in great mis'ry.

I once was His child! What a sweet faded mem'ry!

I fell to my knees; my heart screamed in my chest—oh!

I longed for His love, but knew I deserved death.

It was He that I beat, yes, the King that I cut.

Who could ever forgive me for all that I'd done?

I accepted my fate and prepared for the blow.

"I am ready to die; I have failed you," I choked.

When He lifted my chin, my heart froze in surprise

Because all that I found was pure love in His eyes!

Then He knelt beside me—pulled me into His arms

I collapsed in His grasp; His warmth melted my heart.

Peace enveloped me as He healed all my pain.

With the love of His touch, He had banished my shame.

My words fail to describe the great joy that was known

When He whispered to me, "My dear child, welcome home."

Dragons

I wrote this spoken word when I was 16 years old in January of 2015. I created it specifically for the Fine Arts Festival. I won first place with it at districts. I also performed it at numerous other venues, including open mics and church services.

I am a dragon

Fire raging from my throat

But I didn't even know it

Until I met

One of my victims

I burned rivers

Into her face

And through the tears

Saw my reflection

That I

Was a monster to be feared

I cut down the weak

Thinking it would bring me strength

I was an uncontrollable

Beast

A wild fire blazing

In me

But this wasn't who

I wanted to be

This wasn't the legacy

I wanted to lead

So I became disgusted

With myself

And self-contempt

Boiled within

'Til I was made

My own victim

I burned myself deep

Thinking maybe

I'd be free

But the scales

All too quickly grew

So that no one knew

That on the inside

I was still bleeding

I was still seething

And I was still burning

With self-hate

One day

I encountered The Creator

Walking by

I asked Him why

He cursed me

Why I was doomed

To be used

For destruction

And devastation

Why He bothered making

Such a disgusting

Creation

He looked at me

With eyes of deepest sympathy

In a truest sincerity

He said to me:

"The fire of a dragon

Is not a curse.

You have power

To change the world;

You are of great worth.

Your fire

Is a gift to be used

As a weapon or a tool.

The choice is up to you.

What do you choose?"

It dawned on me

In a light

Far brighter

Than the sun

That the power

Of life and death

Burns upon my tongue

And I am a chosen one

Given gifts and abilities

Of which

Others could only dream

I just didn't know

How to use them

Not comprehending my power

In the past

I abused it

But not anymore

From that day forward

I began training

I learned when to burn bright

And when to contain it

He taught me how

To give light

To the darkest soul

And warm hearts

Suffering

From the severest cold

He told

Me to love my self

Embrace my wings

And embrace my fire

Now my heart of embers

Burns

And soars higher

Than any eagle

More freely than any sparrow

I guide the lost

To the truly safe

But narrow

Path

With my fire

I burn into stone

My testimony

For all to see

Hoping they too

Will choose

To be free

From what cages them

With my flames

I melt the chains

Of prisoners

And the warmth of my fire

Changes them

I once was a weapon

Who knew only how to bring death and

Pain

But I switched sides

And now I

Am a chosen warrior

And bringing life and light

Is my campaign

This is the story

Of a girl

Who once was a monster

But The Creator

Saved her

And taught her

The power of her words

He said:

"Sticks and stones may break bones,

But your words penetrate.

Will you kill or will you save?

On hollow bones,

Your ink will be

What's engraved.

What will you say?"

I ask you

What will you say?

Seasons Change

I wrote this poem when I was 16 years old in response to the changes in my life. I wrote it from the perspective of God speaking to me, His child.

People come and go like the raging tide

But that doesn't mean you should stay inside

And not live your life

You must learn to live in the moment

And enjoy My presence.

People are gifts to be treasured

Not lengths of friendship to be measured

You do not know what tomorrow will bring

Right now is where you are

And you should be free

Stop caging yourself

Because you're afraid of hurting

You always worry about your future

And it has become your burden

I control who will come and go

You must love and hope

And know that I know

That you hurt when people leave

But I am able to heal you

Don't miss out on life's opportunities

Right now is not the end

But a new journey

People's lives are intertwined

Only I know where they'll go

Please trust that the plans I have for you

Are plans filled with hope

I know that you love them

And that it hurts to be open

I didn't ask you to love

So that you would be broken

But so that I could fix you

I needed to teach you

That at times it's easier not to love

But it's never really better

People will come and go

Like the changes of the weather

However, you cannot live alone

I created people to be together

Follow My lead and choose to trust Me

I know at times it hurts and the pain is ugly

But growing pains must happen

So I can make something – Beautiful.

Dear Woman

I wrote this spoken word when I was 16 years old. I created it for a women's event on October 24th, 2015. I centered my piece around the event theme of "Conqueror" by writing to a Dear Woman, who is my mother.

Dear Godly Woman

How I need you in my life!

So often have I

Struggled

In this time of growth

I would be so lost

If you had not shown

Me the way—If

You had not shown me

The greatness

Of the definition of **"Woman"**

Dear Woman

You taught me creativity

And wonder

And to think of God as bowling

Every time I heard thunder

And every lightning meant a strike

So now I spend my time

Outside the box

85

Thinking odd

Yet extraordinary thoughts

Dear Woman

When you taught me how to swim

I learned to never quit

Sometimes I'll feel the pain

Of chlorine in my eyes

But it won't compare

To the feeling of victory

When I can jump off the high dive

I learned that if the prize

Is worth it

I must be determined

Dear Woman

When I assumed my bully was a monster

With a cold heart

You showed me that she felt pain

And that her ache

Reached to the stars

You told me not to judge

A book by its cover

Or even by its prologue

Because though I may see part

Of who she is now

I don't know the burden

She's brought

I don't know the battles

She's faced

So though it seems unfair

I need to give grace

Now

When someone cuts me

I know that with the little that I bleed

They feel

Much more grief

And my kindness might be

The key

That will release

The chains that bind them

Dear Woman

You taught me what honesty is

To let my no be no

And my yes be yes

And there isn't a need

For pinky promises

On my behalf

Because truth

Is the only language I should have

Dear Woman

You showed me sacrifice

By staying by my side

Even though it inhibited your freedom

You stayed

Worked and slaved

To raise me in a way

That would honor God's kingdom

Dear Woman

You showed me

What it is to be a servant

At times

So much is given to you

Yet

You endure it

Embrace it

And face it

With bravery

You comply

With what is asked of you

Even when it's things

You shouldn't have to do

And you do it gracefully

Dear Woman

I learned from you

That "I Do"

Is easier said than done

And that marriage isn't always

All bliss and fun

The media portrays marriage

As a fairy tale

Yet fails to tell

That every fantasy

Has its ups and downs

And you have to learn how

To forgive and be forgiven

And fight

For a life

Worth living

But if done correctly

Though the struggle is real

God works it out

Perfectly

Dear Woman

You taught me perseverance

When you were falsely accused

You said,

"God is my defense"

I could not comprehend

The serenity in your appearance

And how you could ask me

To forgive them

Because "they know not what they do"

You said "God has given me and ever-expanding heart;

He will give me ever-expanding shoulders too"

I watched amazed

As you carried the weight

Through the race

Even though trial

Was all you seemed to face

And in this

You showed me how to carry myself with grace

And humility

And to have faith

That when no one is on my side

God still remains for me

When all else fails

He is still succeeding

Dear Woman

Your passion for God

Is clear and true

It shines through everything you do

Yes!

You love God with all your being

Like Ruth

I have followed your leading

Seeing

The joy and satisfaction

That you find in Him

Though in my youth

I choose to live a life

Patterned after you

Dear Women

Please don't underestimate

Your sphere of influence

Young girls are watching

Everything you're doing

You may say

"I am inadequate.

I have sin and flaws"

Yes

But when you fall

Be brave

And get back up again

Because every champion

Was once defeated

And every warrior

Has her weakness

Yes,

Every champion

Was once defeated

And every warrior

Has her weakness

But the conqueror

Is the Dear Woman

Who does not stay down

But trusts God

Lets Him lift her head

And adjust her crown

Dear Woman

I am not calling you to perfection

But faithfulness

To fight this battle

With your God-given skills

And gracefulness

I am calling you

To lead the charge

To be the conquerors

I know you are.

Caterpillars and Cocoons

I wrote this poem when I was 17 years old. It is the sequel to "Seasons Change."

When you left

I thought it was the end of me

I swore you were what I would always need

As you were ripped away

I feared you were my lost piece

But in reality, you became a warm, sweet memory

Stirred by a spring breeze

As you fell away, I began to shift and grow

More than you know

I now have wings and fly!

I am free and light-spirited like clouds in the sky

I must now reintroduce myself

Me, you may not recognize

There is a wilder love in my eyes

My colors burn brighter and my countenance is lighter

I have a deeper wisdom and respect

I have transformed even more than you may detect

By letting go of you, whom I held so tight

I shed my cocoon and took on flight

You were a shield that I needed in past moments

You proved to me that passion and bravery still exist

As the seasons turned and called you away

I was so afraid to let go

You were a one-of-a-kind friend

I feared I would never again know

I held so tight, but realized it only cut me

It was only when I let go that I could be complete

Seeing you now, dear friend, brings me joy and happiness

It reminds me of how much I've grown

And how far I've rose

On this ever ascending climb

So thank you, my friend, for loving and leaving

Because I have learned how to fly.

Good Enough

I wrote this spoken word when I was 17 years old in January of 2016. Lauren Westlake requested that I create this piece for "Purpose," Native Youth Kansas City's first girls' event. I performed it at multiple women's events. I also took it to the 2016 Fine Arts Festival Districts and won the merit award (first place) in the spoken word category. I also performed "Good Enough" at the National Fine Arts Festival and won third place.

How many times

Do you find

Yourself staring

At your reflection

Seeing

Every imperfection

And flaw

And all

You can think about

Is how

You would change?

You just want

To be *good enough*

If only your hair

Was straight

Your skin

Soft to the touch

Your awkwardness

You would erase

And your dorky laugh

You would trade

For any other

Why

Do you desire

To be

"Something other"

How can you be so unsatisfied

With your life

That you always long

For another's?

I mean yes

That girl is beautiful

But why

Has it become your usual

To want to be

Someone else?

Why is it

That when you are asked,

"What is beautiful?"

You never point to yourself?

You may say,

"Because that is arrogant

And conceited"

But what you don't realize

Is that's a lie

You've been fed

And you believed it

You see

The enemy of your soul

Wants to blindfold

You

So that you mistake

Confidence

For arrogance

And so forget

The truth

That you

Are

Beautiful.

You

Are like a sunrise

Extravagant

In its color

Brilliant

Breathtaking

And unlike

Any other

Your smile

Is a door

Through which the beauty

Of your heart escapes

And dances on your face

Your laugh

Is a song

A chime

A flare at night—Bright

Pointing

To the beauty

And light

Inside you

Your hair is tailor-made

Each stand

Whether straight

Or waved

Whether wild or tamed

Was given to you

Intentionally

And it fits you

Perfectly

Your personality

May be chill

Or high strung

Curious

Ridiculous

Awkward

Intelligent

Or what appears

To be a hot mess

To some

But the way

You dance through life

The world only gets

To see once

You are not an accident

Or a mistaken

Conglomeration

Of strangeness

You are a noble daughter

Of the High King

And He sees

You as His precious

Jewel

You may have

Rough edges

But only a fool

Could deny your worth

You are a unique

And vibrant cord

Woven

Into God's tapestry

Purposed and fashioned

As a portion

Of His masterpiece

Yes!

Joy and compassion

Spill from His heart

Because you are not solely

A piece of art

But His

Beloved daughter

And even angels

Will falter

When you realize

Your value and purpose

You are the only one like you

On earth—this

Is the time

And you must stand out

Look at Esther

Ruth

And Mary

As examples of how

A single woman

Though seemingly

Insignificant

Can make the difference

For generations

To come

By being herself

Even if it means

She's the only one

Dear sister,

You are an unusual

Rare form

Of beautiful

Put God first and

Walk in His purpose

And know

That you are loved

And when you look

In the mirror

Know that you are far more

Than *good enough.*

Anger Management

I wrote this satirical quip when I was 17 years old. I created it in efforts to tolerate an irritating individual by enjoying the good times.

It was good

To see you laugh

It was joy

To see you smile

For I know you've felt pressure and stress for a while

It was good

To see your heart

Rising up to your cheeks

It was nice

To hear your laugh

Every time you would speak

It was good

To see your joy

My heart leapt

To see you free

Can I give you this peace for you always to keep?

Your joy gives me joy

And I smile when you laugh

I'll treasure this time

In my mind when I'm mad.

Like You Love Me

I wrote this rap when I was 17 years old. I performed it to "Falling into You" by Hillsong Young and Free *with the Native Youth Kansas City Worship Team.*

I wanna love you like you love me

Heart open wide

That's who I'm made to be

Perfect Love drove out my fear

Playlist of love songs

Is all that I hear

So let's go for a drive

Turn up the tunes

'Cause my future is bright

Love broke through the storm

Now all I see is a forecast of shine

Farewell for Now

I wrote this spoken word when I was 17 years old. Karen and Ashley Griffin requested that I create this piece to honor Jimmie Ann Griffin, who went to be with the Lord on May 10, 2016. I performed it at Jimmie's celebration of life service on June 6, 2016.

When Jimmie Ann Griffin

Was described to me

I saw her similarity

To the woman in Proverbs 31

I saw her hands

Skilled in their craft

Weaving

Sewing

Rarely idle in her lap

I saw her with arms wide open

Hoping

To help those in need

Who came her way

She desired to lighten their burdens

And ease their pain

I saw wisdom

And understanding

In her eyes

She recognized

The brevity of this life

She was aware

Of her spiritual race

And did not chase

Worldly pleasures

But pursued

The true treasure

That only comes

From One

Jesus Christ

God's only Son

I saw a faithful woman

Who served the Lord

While defiantly

Diverging

From the ways

Of the world

In her life

She set her eyes

On the prize

In the end

Her flesh was weak

But her spirit was strong

So she achieved that

For which her spirit longed

She is at peace

Body and soul

She laughs

At her life's trials

Because they could not keep her

From her goal

Now she's dancing

With God Himself

She has joy in her heart

And perfect health

Her hands

No longer ache

And her heart

No longer breaks

With the pain

Of this place

Rather

She is caught

In His gaze

Standing

Face to face

With her Maker

She knows True Love

And He knows her

Her eyes

Are filled with light

For she has seen The One

Who gives life

Jubilee

Is her companion

And laughter

Is her friend

She's dancing to jazz

With God in heaven

She's happy

She's whole

And she wants you

To feel this too

Because though

For a time she is gone

She knows

She'll see you soon

Then you'll dance and laugh

In God's grace

Giving Him praise

And glorifying His Name

But until that day

You must run your race

Following

The example she gave

Knowing that

"To live is Christ

But to die is gain"

I understand

You are in pain

And there is a hurt

In your heart

But don't forget

To run to God

Where He will hold

You in His arms

He'll bottle your tears

And replace them with the hope

Saying, "Soon,

We'll all be together

In heaven

Our home."

The Black and White Fallacy

I wrote this rap when I was 17 years old in response to the deaths of Alton Sterling and Philando Castile.

Another day

Another shooting

Welcome to the U.S.A.

Full of Confusion

They say a house divided

Will fall

Well call

"Timber!"

Because this crash

Will kill us all

Justice escapes

And accountability

Is fleeting

Blood bathes the streets

Leaving moms

And kids screaming

The situation isn't black and white

There are deep hues of gray

Smeared with blood

From every fight

The past two nights

We lost two more lives.

There's the question in the air,

"Were they given their rights?"

I don't know if they were innocent

But would there be different

Consequences given them

If they were white?

I don't know if you follow me

All I really want is equality

Not exemption from the law

But protection from all

The perpetuators of this

Black and White fallacy.